Salmon

Recipes

Introduction

Salmon is one of the most versatile and nutritious fish in the world, and this cookbook celebrates its delicious and healthy qualities. With its distinctive pink flesh and rich, buttery flavor, salmon is enjoyed by people all over the world and is often considered a delicacy.

Not only is salmon a delicious addition to any meal, but it is also packed with essential nutrients and vitamins, making it a great choice for a healthy and balanced diet. It is an excellent source of high-quality protein, omega-3 fatty acids, vitamin D, and B vitamins, making it a great choice for anyone looking to improve their health.

From grilled and baked to smoked and fried, there are countless ways to prepare and enjoy salmon. This cookbook features a range of recipes that showcase the versatility and flavor of this incredible fish, from simple and quick weeknight dinners to impressive dishes perfect for entertaining.

Whether you are a seasoned chef or a novice in the kitchen, this cookbook is the perfect guide for anyone looking to explore the world of salmon and take their cooking skills to the next level. So grab your apron and get ready to discover the delicious and nutritious world of salmon cuisine!

Different Types of Salmon

According to the National Oceanic and Atmospheric Administration, salmon is the most popular seafood species in the U.S., with a commercial value of $688 million in 2017, due to its health benefits and high levels of omega-3 fatty acids. However, not all salmon is the same, and there are six types of commercially available salmon in the U.S., such as Sockeye and King salmon. To help clarify the differences between these types, it's important to first understand how salmon is raised.

Farmed vs. Wild Salmon

Wild salmon is caught in natural environments such as oceans, rivers, and lakes, while farmed salmon is a prevalent option globally. Fish farms utilize aquaculture to breed fish and usually feed them processed diets that are high in fat and protein, which results in larger fish. The nutrient composition of wild and farmed salmon differs significantly due to their distinct diets. Wild salmon contains more minerals, whereas farmed salmon is richer in vitamin C, calories, and saturated fat.

Research suggests that farmed salmon may contain higher levels of contaminants compared to wild salmon. Although both types are good sources of omega-3s, wild salmon is the better option for overall health, albeit pricier.

Pacific salmon, including King, Sockeye, Coho, Pink, and Chum, are the five types of wild salmon to opt for. Atlantic salmon is not inferior to Pacific salmon, but they are mainly farm-raised, given the scarcity of wild Atlantic salmon due to overfishing and habitat destruction. Check out the following article to learn more about the six common types of salmon.

Chinook or King Salmon

With its regal title, King salmon, also known as Chinook, is often regarded as the finest salmon variety available. It is rich, large, and high in fat, making it a great source of omega-3s.

King salmon can grow up to five feet in length and exceed 100 pounds in weight, thriving in Pacific waters from southern California to the icy rivers of northern Alaska.

Sockeye or Red Salmon

Sockeye, also called Red salmon, is recognized for its distinctive reddish-orange flesh and pungent odor. It's known to have a more robust, fishier flavor.

Compared to King salmon, Sockeye salmon is smaller, leaner, and more affordable. These salmon are frequently sold smoked and are highly regarded by chefs nationwide. They're named for their bright red flesh, and their skin turns a deep red as they swim upstream to spawn. Sockeye salmon is mostly found in Alaskan waters.

Coho or Silver Salmon

Silver or Coho salmon are identified by their gleaming silver skin. Despite not being as famous as the larger King or more flavorful Sockeye varieties, Coho salmon have moderate fat content and a gentler taste.

Due to their smaller size, Coho salmon are frequently utilized when cooking a whole salmon. Their flavor is comparable to Kings, but with a more delicate texture. They are typically caught in Alaskan waters and throughout the northern Pacific.

Pink or Humpback Salmon

Pink or Humpback salmon are characterized by a notable hump on their back that develops when they spawn, which is why they're also called "humpies". They have a light-colored flesh and a mild flavor with low fat content. These salmon are typically small in size, weighing between two and six pounds.

Although fresh and frozen Pink salmon can be found, they are more commonly processed and sold in cans or pouches. Most Pink salmon is sourced from Alaskan fisheries, but they can also be found along the coasts of Washington and Oregon. Fun fact: In 2017, U.S. fishermen harvested more Pink salmon than any other fish, totaling 495 million pounds.

Chum, Silverbrite, Keta or Dog

Chum salmon goes by many names. This light to medium-colored fish has a lower fat content and smaller size. It's flesh is often sold canned or frozen.

However, it does have one big thing going for it: its roe. Roe, or fish eggs contained in the ovaries of a female fish, is considered a delicacy in many cuisines. Chum's roe is often bigger and tastier than other types of salmon. It's often used for Ikura (salmon caviar).

Chum salmon is mostly harvested from Alaskan waters. Chum salmon is also known as Silverbrite, Keta, or Dog salmon due to its light to medium-colored flesh and smaller size with lower fat content. Its flesh is usually sold frozen or canned. However, it is popularly known for its roe which is larger and more flavorful than other types of salmon. Chum salmon roe is widely used in various cuisines, especially in making salmon caviar or Ikura. Most of the chum salmon is harvested from Alaskan waters.

Atlantic or Salmo Salar

The Atlantic salmon, scientifically known as Salmo salar, is the only salmon species that is not native to the Pacific Ocean. Nevertheless, all the Atlantic salmon available in the market are farmed as only a few endangered wild populations remain. Compared to other salmon types, Atlantic salmon is usually larger in size due to their specialized diet and has a milder taste.

Fish farming practices are starting to shift towards more sustainable plant-based feeds. Thus, there are ongoing efforts to improve fish farming practices for Atlantic salmon. Since it is farm-raised, Atlantic salmon is generally more affordable than most wild-caught salmon.

Classic Salmon Cakes

Ingredients:

2 cans of salmon, drained and flaked
1/2 cup breadcrumbs
1/4 cup mayonnaise
1 egg, beaten
1/4 cup chopped onion
2 tbsps. chopped fresh parsley
1 tsp. Dijon mustard
Salt and pepper to taste
2 tbsps. olive oil

Directions:

1. In a large mixing bowl, combine the salmon, breadcrumbs, mayonnaise, egg, onion, parsley, Dijon mustard, salt, and pepper.
2. Mix well.
3. Form the mixture into patties.
4. Heat the olive oil in a large skillet over medium-high heat.
5. Add the patties and cook until golden brown, about 3-4 minutes per side.
6. Serve hot.

Asian Salmon Cakes

Ingredients:

2 cans of salmon, drained and flaked
1/2 cup panko breadcrumbs
1/4 cup soy sauce
2 tbsps. rice vinegar
2 tbsps. chopped green onions
1 tbsp. grated ginger
1 tbsp. sesame oil
1 egg, beaten
Salt and pepper to taste
2 tbsps. vegetable oil

Directions:

1. In a large mixing bowl, combine the salmon, panko breadcrumbs, soy sauce, rice vinegar, green onions, ginger, sesame oil, egg, salt, and pepper.
2. Mix well.
3. Form the mixture into patties.
4. Heat the vegetable oil in a large skillet over medium-high heat.
5. Add the patties and cook until golden brown, about 3-4 minutes per side.
6. Serve hot.

Sweet Potato Salmon Cakes

Ingredients:

2 cans of salmon, drained and flaked
1 medium sweet potato, peeled and grated
1/4 cup almond flour
2 tbsps. chopped fresh chives
1 egg, beaten
1 tbsp. Dijon mustard
Salt and pepper to taste
2 tbsps. coconut oil

Directions:

1. In a large mixing bowl, combine the salmon, sweet potato, almond flour, chives, egg, Dijon mustard, salt, and pepper.
2. Mix well.
3. Form the mixture into patties.
4. Heat the coconut oil in a large skillet over medium-high heat.
5. Add the patties and cook until golden brown, about 3-4 minutes per side.
6. Serve hot.

Quinoa Salmon Cakes

Ingredients:

2 cans of salmon, drained and flaked
1 cup cooked quinoa
1/4 cup breadcrumbs
1/4 cup chopped fresh cilantro
1 egg, beaten
1 tbsp. lime juice
1 tsp. cumin
Salt and pepper to taste
2 tbsps. olive oil

Directions:

1. In a large mixing bowl, combine the salmon, quinoa, breadcrumbs, cilantro, egg, lime juice, cumin, salt, and pepper.
2. Mix well.
3. Form the mixture into patties.
4. Heat the olive oil in a large skillet over medium-high heat.
5. Add the patties and cook until golden brown, about 3-4 minutes per side.
6. Serve hot.

Italian Salmon Cakes

Ingredients:

2 cans of salmon, drained and flaked
1/2 cup breadcrumbs
1/4 cup grated Parmesan cheese
1/4 cup chopped fresh basil
1 egg, beaten
1 tbsp. lemon juice
1 tsp. dried oregano
Salt and pepper to taste
2 tbsps. olive oil

Directions:

1. In a large mixing bowl, combine the salmon, breadcrumbs, Parmesan cheese, basil, egg, lemon juice, oregano, salt, and pepper.
2. Mix well.
3. Form the mixture into patties.
4. Heat the olive oil in a large skillet over medium-high heat.
5. Add the patties and cook until golden brown, about 3-4 minutes per side.
6. Serve hot with a side of marinara sauce or lemon wedges. Enjoy!

Classic Smoked Salmon Dip:

Ingredients:

8 oz. smoked salmon, chopped
8 oz. cream cheese, softened
1/4 cup sour cream
1/4 cup mayonnaise
1 tbsp fresh dill, chopped
1 tbsp lemon juice
Salt and pepper to taste

Directions:

1. Mix all the ingredients together in a bowl until well combined.
2. Chill in the refrigerator for at least an hour before serving.
3. Serve with crackers or sliced baguette.

Smoked Salmon Dip with Horseradish:

Ingredients:

8 oz. smoked salmon, chopped
8 oz. cream cheese, softened
1/4 cup sour cream
1/4 cup mayonnaise
1 tbsp fresh dill, chopped
1 tbsp lemon juice
2 tbsp prepared horseradish
Salt and pepper to taste

Directions:

1. Mix all the ingredients together in a bowl until well combined.
2. Chill in the refrigerator for at least an hour before serving.
3. Serve with crackers or sliced baguette.

Smoked Salmon Dip with Greek Yogurt:

Ingredients:

8 oz. smoked salmon, chopped
8 oz. Greek yogurt
1/4 cup mayonnaise
1 tbsp fresh dill, chopped
1 tbsp lemon juice
Salt and pepper to taste

Directions:

1. Mix all the ingredients together in a bowl until well combined.
2. Chill in the refrigerator for at least an hour before serving.
3. Serve with cucumber slices or pita chips.

Smoked Salmon Dip with Cream Cheese and Capers

Ingredients:

8 oz. smoked salmon, chopped
8 oz. cream cheese, softened
1/4 cup sour cream
1/4 cup mayonnaise
1 tbsp fresh dill, chopped
1 tbsp lemon juice
2 tbsp capers, drained
Salt and pepper to taste

Directions:

1. Mix all the ingredients together in a bowl until well combined.
2. Chill in the refrigerator for at least an hour before serving.
3. Serve with toast points or sliced baguette.

Smoked Salmon Dip with Avocado:

Ingredients:

8 oz. smoked salmon, chopped
1 ripe avocado, mashed
1/4 cup sour cream
1/4 cup mayonnaise
1 tbsp fresh dill, chopped
1 tbsp lemon juice
Salt and pepper to taste

Directions:

1. Mix all the ingredients together in a bowl until well combined.
2. Chill in the refrigerator for at least an hour before serving.
3. Serve with tortilla chips or sliced vegetables.

Creamy Salmon Chowder

Ingredients:

2 tbsp butter
1 onion, chopped
1 cup celery, chopped
1 cup carrots, chopped
3 cups chicken broth
2 cups potatoes, peeled and diced
1 tsp dried thyme
1 bay leaf
1 lb cooked salmon, flaked
2 cups heavy cream
Salt and pepper to taste

Directions:

1. Melt butter in a large pot over medium heat.
2. Add onion, celery, and carrots and sauté until tender.
3. Add chicken broth, potatoes, thyme, and bay leaf.
4. Bring to a boil, then reduce heat and simmer until potatoes are tender.
5. Remove bay leaf and stir in salmon and heavy cream.
6. Season with salt and pepper to taste.
7. Simmer for an additional 5-10 minutes until heated through.
8. Serve hot.

Smoked Salmon Chowder

Ingredients:

2 tbsp butter
1 onion, chopped
3 cloves garlic, minced
1 cup celery, chopped
1 cup carrots, chopped
2 cups chicken broth
2 cups potatoes, peeled and diced
1 tsp dried thyme
1 bay leaf
1 lb smoked salmon, flaked
2 cups half-and-half
Salt and pepper to taste

Directions:

1. Melt butter in a large pot over medium heat.
2. Add onion, garlic, celery, and carrots and sauté until tender.
3. Add chicken broth, potatoes, thyme, and bay leaf.
4. Bring to a boil, then reduce heat and simmer until potatoes are tender.
5. Remove bay leaf and stir in smoked salmon and half-and-half.
6. Season with salt and pepper to taste.
7. Simmer for an additional 5-10 minutes until heated through.
8. Serve hot.

Spicy Salmon Chowder

Ingredients:

2 tbsp olive oil
1 onion, chopped
2 cloves garlic, minced
1 cup celery, chopped
1 cup carrots, chopped
3 cups chicken broth
2 cups potatoes, peeled and diced
1 tsp dried thyme
1 bay leaf
1 lb cooked salmon, flaked
1 cup corn kernels
1 cup half-and-half
1 tbsp hot sauce
Salt and pepper to taste

Directions:

1. Heat olive oil in a large pot over medium heat.
2. Add onion, garlic, celery, and carrots and sauté until tender.
3. Add chicken broth, potatoes, thyme, and bay leaf.
4. Bring to a boil, then reduce heat and simmer until potatoes are tender.
5. Remove bay leaf and stir in salmon, corn, half-and-half, and hot sauce.
6. Season with salt and pepper to taste.
7. Simmer for an additional 5-10 minutes until heated through.
8. Serve hot.
9. Salmon Salad
10. : Mix flaked salmon with chopped celery, red onion, mayonnaise, Dijon mustard, and lemon juice.
11. Serve on a bed of lettuce or in a sandwich.

Classic Salmon Salad

Ingredients:

2 (6-oz.) cans of salmon, drained and flaked
1/2 cup mayonnaise
2 tbsps. fresh lemon juice
1/4 cup finely chopped red onion
1/4 cup finely chopped celery
Salt and black pepper, to taste
Lettuce leaves, for serving

Directions:

1. In a large bowl, combine the salmon, mayonnaise, lemon juice, red onion, and celery.
2. Mix well.
3. Season with salt and black pepper, to taste.
4. Serve on top of lettuce leaves.

Avocado Salmon Salad

Ingredients:

2 (6-oz.) cans of salmon, drained and flaked
1 ripe avocado, peeled and mashed
2 tbsps. Greek yogurt
2 tbsps. chopped fresh cilantro
2 tsps. lime juice
Salt and black pepper, to taste
Mixed greens, for serving

Directions:

1. In a large bowl, combine the salmon, mashed avocado, Greek yogurt, cilantro, and lime juice.
2. Mix well.
3. Season with salt and black pepper, to taste.
4. Serve on top of mixed greens.

Salmon and Quinoa Salad

Ingredients:

1 cup cooked quinoa
2 (6-oz.) cans of salmon, drained and flaked
1/2 cup chopped cucumber
1/2 cup chopped cherry tomatoes
1/4 cup chopped red onion
2 tbsps. chopped fresh parsley
2 tbsps. olive oil
1 tbsp. red wine vinegar
Salt and black pepper, to taste

Directions:

1. In a large bowl, combine the cooked quinoa, salmon, cucumber, cherry tomatoes, red onion, and parsley.
2. Mix well.
3. In a separate small bowl, whisk together the olive oil and red wine vinegar.
4. Pour the dressing over the salad and mix well.
5. Season with salt and black pepper, to taste.

Sesame Ginger Salmon Salad

Ingredients:

2 (6-oz.) cans of salmon, drained and flaked
1/2 cup shredded carrots
1/2 cup shredded red cabbage
1/4 cup chopped scallions
2 tbsps. chopped fresh cilantro
2 tbsps. sesame oil
1 tbsp. rice vinegar
1 tbsp. soy sauce
1 tsp. grated ginger
Salt and black pepper, to taste

Directions:

1. In a large bowl, combine the salmon, shredded carrots, shredded red cabbage, scallions, and cilantro.
2. Mix well.
3. In a separate small bowl, whisk together the sesame oil, rice vinegar, soy sauce, and grated ginger.
4. Pour the dressing over the salad and mix well.
5. Season with salt and black pepper, to taste.

Asian Salmon Salad

Ingredients:

1 lb. salmon fillet, skin removed
4 cups mixed salad greens
1 cup shredded carrots
1 cup sliced cucumbers
1 cup cherry tomatoes, halved
1 avocado, sliced
1/4 cup chopped cilantro
1/4 cup chopped green onions
1/4 cup toasted sesame seeds

Dressing Ingredients:

2 tbsp. soy sauce
2 tbsp. rice vinegar
1 tbsp. honey
1 tbsp. sesame oil
1 tbsp. grated ginger
1 garlic clove, minced
Salt and pepper to taste

Directions:

1. Preheat oven to 375 degrees F.
2. Season the salmon with salt and pepper, and bake for 12-15 minutes or until fully cooked.
3. Let the salmon cool, then flake into bite-sized pieces.
4. In a large bowl, mix together the salad greens, carrots, cucumbers, cherry tomatoes, avocado, cilantro, and green onions.
5. In a small bowl, whisk together the soy sauce, rice vinegar, honey, sesame oil, ginger, garlic, salt, and pepper to make the dressing.
6. Add the salmon to the salad and drizzle with the dressing.
7. Toss until well combined.
8. Garnish with toasted sesame seeds and serve.

Grilled Peach and Salmon Salad

Ingredients:

1 lb. salmon fillet, skin removed
4 cups mixed salad greens
2 ripe peaches, sliced
1/4 cup crumbled feta cheese
1/4 cup chopped fresh mint
1/4 cup chopped almonds

Dressing Ingredients:

1/4 cup olive oil
2 tbsp. white balsamic vinegar
1 tbsp. honey
1 tsp. Dijon mustard
Salt and pepper to taste

Directions:

1. Preheat grill to medium-high heat.
2. Season the salmon with salt and pepper, and grill for 5-6 minutes per side or until fully cooked.
3. Let the salmon cool, then flake into bite-sized pieces.
4. In a large bowl, mix together the salad greens, sliced peaches, crumbled feta cheese, and chopped mint.
5. In a small bowl, whisk together the olive oil, white balsamic vinegar, honey, Dijon mustard, salt, and pepper to make the dressing.
6. Add the salmon to the salad and drizzle with the dressing.
7. Toss until well combined.
8. Garnish with chopped almonds and serve.

Greek Salmon Salad

Ingredients:

1 lb cooked salmon, flaked
1/2 red onion, thinly sliced
1 cucumber, diced
1 cup cherry tomatoes, halved
1/2 cup pitted kalamata olives, halved
1/2 cup crumbled feta cheese
1/4 cup chopped fresh parsley
1/4 cup chopped fresh dill
1/4 cup olive oil
2 tbsp red wine vinegar
1 clove garlic, minced
Salt and pepper, to taste

Directions:

1. In a large bowl, combine the flaked salmon, red onion, cucumber, cherry tomatoes, olives, feta cheese, parsley, and dill.
2. In a small bowl, whisk together the olive oil, red wine vinegar, garlic, salt, and pepper.
3. Pour the dressing over the salmon mixture and toss to coat evenly.
4. Serve immediately or chill until ready to serve.

Teriyaki Salmon Stir-Fry

Ingredients:

1 lb salmon fillet, skin removed and cut into bite-sized pieces
1 tbsp vegetable oil
1 red bell pepper, sliced
1 green bell pepper, sliced
1 yellow onion, sliced
2 cloves garlic, minced
1/4 cup teriyaki sauce
2 tbsp honey
1 tsp sesame oil
1/4 cup chopped scallions

Directions:

1. In a large skillet or wok, heat the vegetable oil over high heat.
2. Add the salmon and cook for 3-4 minutes or until browned on all sides.
3. Remove from pan and set aside.
4. Add the bell peppers and onion to the pan and stir-fry for 2-3 minutes.
5. Add the garlic and stir-fry for an additional minute.
6. In a small bowl, whisk together the teriyaki sauce, honey, and sesame oil.
7. Return the salmon to the pan and pour the teriyaki mixture over the top.
8. Stir-fry for an additional 2-3 minutes, or until the sauce has thickened and the salmon is cooked through.
9. Serve hot, garnished with chopped scallions.

Spicy Salmon and Broccoli Stir-Fry

Ingredients:

1 lb salmon fillet, skin removed and cut into bite-sized pieces
2 tbsp vegetable oil
1 head broccoli, cut into florets
1 red bell pepper, sliced
2 cloves garlic, minced
1 tbsp soy sauce
1 tbsp oyster sauce
1 tbsp chili garlic sauce
1 tsp sesame oil
1/4 cup chopped cilantro

Directions:

1. In a large skillet or wok, heat the vegetable oil over high heat.
2. Add the salmon and cook for 3-4 minutes or until browned on all sides.
3. Remove from pan and set aside.
4. Add the broccoli and bell pepper to the pan and stir-fry for 2-3 minutes.
5. Add the garlic and stir-fry for an additional minute.
6. In a small bowl, whisk together the soy sauce, oyster sauce, chili garlic sauce, and sesame oil.
7. Return the salmon to the pan and pour the sauce over the top.
8. Stir-fry for an additional 2-3 minutes, or until the sauce has thickened and the salmon is cooked through.
9. Serve hot, garnished with chopped cilantro.

Salmon and Asparagus Stir-Fry

Ingredients:

1 lb salmon fillet, skin removed and cut into bite-sized pieces
1 bunch asparagus, tough ends trimmed and cut into 2-inch pieces
1 red bell pepper, seeded and thinly sliced
1 tbsp. ginger, grated
3 garlic cloves, minced
2 tbsps. soy sauce
1 tbsp. honey
1 tbsp. cornstarch
2 tbsps. vegetable oil
Salt and pepper to taste
Cooked rice for serving

Directions:

1. In a small bowl, whisk together soy sauce, honey, and cornstarch until smooth.
2. Set aside.
3. Heat vegetable oil in a large skillet or wok over medium-high heat.
4. Add ginger and garlic and stir-fry for 1 minute.
5. Add salmon and stir-fry for 2-3 minutes until browned.
6. Add asparagus and red bell pepper and stir-fry for another 2-3 minutes until vegetables are tender-crisp.
7. Pour the soy sauce mixture over the salmon and vegetables and stir-fry for 1-2 minutes until the sauce thickens and coats the salmon and vegetables.
8. Season with salt and pepper to taste.
9. Serve hot over cooked rice.

Honey Garlic Salmon Stir-Fry

Ingredients:

1 lb salmon fillet, cut into small cubes
2 cups chopped mixed vegetables (bell peppers, onions, broccoli, carrots, etc.)
3 cloves garlic, minced
2 tbsp honey
2 tbsp soy sauce
1 tbsp rice vinegar
1 tsp sesame oil
1 tbsp cornstarch
1/4 cup water
Salt and pepper to taste
Cooking oil

Directions:

1. In a small bowl, mix together honey, soy sauce, rice vinegar, sesame oil, and cornstarch.
2. Set aside.
3. Season the salmon cubes with salt and pepper.
4. Heat some cooking oil in a wok or large skillet over high heat.
5. Add the salmon cubes and stir-fry for about 2-3 minutes, until lightly browned on all sides.
6. Remove from pan and set aside.
7. In the same pan, add more oil if needed and stir-fry the mixed vegetables for about 2-3 minutes.
8. Add the minced garlic and stir-fry for another 30 seconds.
9. Add the cooked salmon back to the pan and pour in the honey garlic sauce.
10. Stir everything together and let it cook for another 2-3 minutes, until the sauce thickens and the salmon is cooked through.
11. Serve hot with steamed rice. Enjoy!

Pineapple and Ginger Salmon Stir-Fry

Ingredients:

1 lb salmon, cut into small pieces
1 red bell pepper, sliced
1 yellow bell pepper, sliced
1 cup fresh pineapple, cubed
2 cloves garlic, minced
1 tbsp. fresh ginger, grated
1 tbsp. cornstarch
1/4 cup soy sauce
1/4 cup pineapple juice
1 tbsp. honey
1 tbsp. vegetable oil
2 green onions, sliced
Salt and pepper, to taste

Directions:

1. In a small bowl, whisk together cornstarch, soy sauce, pineapple juice, honey, and set aside.
2. In a large skillet or wok, heat oil over medium-high heat.
3. Add salmon and stir-fry for 3-4 minutes until browned.
4. Remove from the skillet and set aside.
5. In the same skillet, add bell peppers, pineapple, garlic, and ginger.
6. Stir-fry for 2-3 minutes until vegetables are tender.
7. Pour in the sauce mixture and stir-fry until the sauce has thickened and the vegetables are coated.
8. Add the salmon back to the skillet and stir-fry for another minute until heated through.
9. Season with salt and pepper to taste.
10. Serve hot, garnished with sliced green onions.

Spicy Korean Salmon Stir-Fry

Ingredients:

1 lb salmon fillet, cut into bite-sized pieces
2 tbsp vegetable oil
1/2 onion, sliced
2 garlic cloves, minced
1 inch ginger, peeled and minced
1 red bell pepper, sliced
1 green bell pepper, sliced
2 tbsp gochujang (Korean chili paste)
1 tbsp soy sauce
1 tbsp rice vinegar
1 tbsp honey
1 tsp sesame oil
1 tsp cornstarch
Salt and pepper, to taste
Cooked rice, for serving
Sesame seeds, for garnish

Directions:

1. In a small bowl, whisk together gochujang, soy sauce, rice vinegar, honey, sesame oil, cornstarch, and a pinch of salt and pepper.
2. Set aside.
3. Heat 1 tbsp. of vegetable oil in a wok or large skillet over medium-high heat.
4. Add the salmon and cook for 2-3 minutes on each side, until browned and crispy.
5. Remove from the pan and set aside.
6. Add the remaining tbsp. of oil to the pan, then add the onion, garlic, and ginger.
7. Cook for 1-2 minutes until fragrant.
8. Add the sliced bell peppers and cook for 2-3 minutes until slightly softened.

9. Return the salmon to the pan, then pour the sauce over the salmon and vegetables.
10. Toss to coat everything evenly.
11. Cook for another 2-3 minutes until the sauce has thickened and the salmon is cooked through.
12. Serve over rice and garnish with sesame seeds. Enjoy!

Lemon Herb Salmon Stir-Fry

Ingredients:

1 lb salmon fillet, cut into bite-size pieces
2 tbsps. olive oil
2 cloves garlic, minced
1 tbsp. grated lemon zest
2 tbsps. lemon juice
1 tbsp. chopped fresh parsley
1 tbsp. chopped fresh basil
Salt and pepper, to taste
1 red bell pepper, sliced
1 cup snow peas
1 cup sliced mushrooms
1 tbsp. cornstarch
1/4 cup chicken broth

Directions:

1. Heat the olive oil in a large skillet over medium-high heat.
2. Add the garlic and cook for 30 seconds.
3. Add the salmon, lemon zest, lemon juice, parsley, basil, salt, and pepper.
4. Cook for 3-4 minutes, until the salmon is just cooked through.
5. Remove the salmon from the pan and set aside.
6. Add the red bell pepper, snow peas, and mushrooms to the pan and cook for 2-3 minutes, until slightly softened.
7. Mix the cornstarch and chicken broth together in a small bowl.
8. Add the mixture to the pan and stir until thickened.
9. Add the salmon back to the pan and stir to coat with the sauce.
10. Serve over rice or noodles, if desired.

Thai Basil Salmon Stir-Fry

Ingredients:

1 lb salmon fillet, skin removed and cut into small cubes
2 tbsps. oil
4 garlic cloves, minced
1 red bell pepper, sliced
1 yellow onion, sliced
1 tbsp. soy sauce
1 tbsp. oyster sauce
1 tbsp. fish sauce
1 tsp. sugar
1/2 tsp. black pepper
1/2 cup fresh Thai basil leaves
Cooked jasmine rice, for serving

Directions:

1. Heat the oil in a wok or large skillet over high heat.
2. Add the garlic and cook for 30 seconds until fragrant.
3. Add the salmon and stir-fry for 2-3 minutes until lightly browned.
4. Add the sliced bell pepper and onion and stir-fry for 2-3 minutes until the vegetables are tender-crisp.
5. Add the soy sauce, oyster sauce, fish sauce, sugar, and black pepper, and stir well to combine.
6. Stir in the Thai basil leaves and cook for another 1-2 minutes until the leaves are wilted.
7. Serve the stir-fry over jasmine rice. Enjoy!

Lemon Garlic Baked Salmon

Ingredients:

4 (6 oz) salmon fillets
Salt and pepper
4 cloves garlic, minced
4 tbsp butter, melted
2 tbsp lemon juice
1 tsp lemon zest
2 tbsp chopped parsley

Directions:

1. Preheat oven to 375 degrees F.
2. Place the salmon fillets on a baking sheet lined with parchment paper.
3. Season the salmon with salt and pepper.
4. In a small bowl, combine the minced garlic, melted butter, lemon juice, and lemon zest.
5. Drizzle the mixture over the salmon fillets.
6. Bake the salmon for 15-20 minutes, or until the internal temperature reaches 145 degrees F.
7. Sprinkle chopped parsley on top of the salmon fillets before serving.

Maple Mustard Baked Salmon

Ingredients:

1 lb salmon fillet
2 tbsps. maple syrup
1 tbsp. Dijon mustard
1 tbsp. olive oil
Salt and pepper
2 cloves garlic, minced
Lemon wedges, for serving
Fresh parsley, chopped, for garnish

Directions:

1. Preheat the oven to 375 degrees F (190°C).
2. Line a baking dish with parchment paper.
3. In a small bowl, whisk together the maple syrup, Dijon mustard, olive oil, garlic, salt, and pepper.
4. Place the salmon fillet in the prepared baking dish, skin-side down.
5. Spoon the maple mustard mixture over the salmon, spreading it evenly with a brush or a spoon.
6. Bake the salmon for 15-20 minutes, or until cooked through and flaky.
7. Serve the salmon with lemon wedges and fresh parsley. Enjoy!

Parmesan Crusted Baked Salmon

Ingredients:

4 salmon fillets
1/2 cup grated Parmesan cheese
1/2 cup panko breadcrumbs
2 tbsp chopped fresh parsley
1 tsp garlic powder
1/2 tsp salt
1/4 tsp black pepper
3 tbsp melted butter

Directions:

1. Preheat the oven to 400 degrees F (200°C).
2. Line a baking sheet with parchment paper.
3. In a bowl, combine the Parmesan cheese, panko breadcrumbs, chopped parsley, garlic powder, salt, and pepper.
4. Brush the salmon fillets with melted butter and place them on the prepared baking sheet.
5. Divide the Parmesan mixture evenly over the salmon fillets, pressing it gently to adhere.
6. Bake the salmon for 12-15 minutes, until the crust is golden brown and the salmon is cooked through.
7. Serve hot, garnished with additional chopped parsley if desired. Enjoy!

Mediterranean Baked Salmon

Ingredients:

4 salmon fillets
1/2 cup sun-dried tomatoes
1/4 cup kalamata olives, pitted and chopped
1/4 cup chopped fresh parsley
1/4 cup crumbled feta cheese
2 tbsps. capers, drained
2 cloves garlic, minced
2 tbsps. olive oil
Salt and pepper, to taste
Lemon wedges, for serving

Directions:

1. Preheat the oven to 400 degrees F (200°C).
2. In a small bowl, combine the sun-dried tomatoes, kalamata olives, parsley, feta cheese, capers, and garlic.
3. Set aside.
4. Season the salmon fillets with salt and pepper.
5. Heat the olive oil in a large oven-safe skillet over medium-high heat.
6. Once hot, add the salmon fillets skin-side down and sear for 2-3 minutes until golden brown.
7. Flip the salmon fillets and spoon the sun-dried tomato mixture over the top.
8. Transfer the skillet to the oven and bake for 10-12 minutes or until the salmon is cooked through.
9. Serve hot with lemon wedges. Enjoy!

Teriyaki Baked Salmon

Ingredients:

4 salmon fillets
1/4 cup soy sauce
1/4 cup honey
1/4 cup rice vinegar
1 tbsp. sesame oil
2 garlic cloves, minced
1 tsp. grated fresh ginger
2 tbsps. cornstarch
2 tbsps. water
Sliced green onions and sesame seeds, for garnish

Directions:

1. Preheat the oven to 400 degrees F and line a baking sheet with parchment paper.
2. In a small saucepan, whisk together soy sauce, honey, rice vinegar, sesame oil, garlic, and ginger.
3. Bring to a simmer over medium heat and cook for 3-4 minutes until slightly thickened.
4. In a small bowl, whisk together cornstarch and water to create a slurry.
5. Pour into the soy sauce mixture and whisk until combined. Simmer for an additional 1-2 minutes until the sauce has thickened to your liking.
6. Place the salmon fillets on the prepared baking sheet and brush the teriyaki sauce on top.
7. Bake for 12-15 minutes, or until the salmon is cooked through and flakes easily with a fork.
8. Serve with additional teriyaki sauce and garnish with sliced green onions and sesame seeds. Enjoy!

Herb Butter Baked Salmon

Ingredients:

4 (6-oz.) salmon fillets
1/4 cup unsalted butter, softened
2 garlic cloves, minced
1 tbsp. chopped fresh parsley
1 tbsp. chopped fresh dill
1 tbsp. chopped fresh chives
1/2 tsp. salt
1/4 tsp. black pepper

Directions:

1. Preheat the oven to 400 degrees F (200°C).
2. In a small mixing bowl, stir together the softened butter, minced garlic, chopped parsley, chopped dill, chopped chives, salt, and black pepper.
3. Line a baking sheet with parchment paper and place the salmon fillets on the paper.
4. Spread the herb butter mixture over the top of each fillet, using a rubber spatula to coat evenly.
5. Bake for 12-15 minutes, or until the salmon is cooked through and flakes easily with a fork.
6. Serve immediately and enjoy!

Pesto Baked Salmon

Ingredients:

4 salmon fillets
1/2 cup pesto sauce
1/2 cup breadcrumbs
1/2 cup grated parmesan cheese
Salt and pepper
Lemon wedges (for serving)

Directions:

1. Preheat your oven to 400 degrees F (200°C).
2. Place the salmon fillets on a baking sheet lined with parchment paper.
3. Season the salmon with salt and pepper.
4. Spread the pesto sauce evenly over the salmon fillets.
5. In a small bowl, mix together the breadcrumbs and grated parmesan cheese.
6. Sprinkle the breadcrumb mixture over the pesto-coated salmon fillets, pressing down lightly to adhere.
7. Bake the salmon for 12-15 minutes, or until the fish is cooked through and the topping is golden brown.
8. Serve the salmon with lemon wedges on the side for squeezing over the top.

Honey Mustard Baked Salmon

Ingredients:

4 salmon fillets (about 6 oz each)
1/4 cup honey
1/4 cup dijon mustard
1 tbsp. olive oil
1 tbsp. fresh lemon juice
1 tsp. paprika
Salt and pepper, to taste
Lemon wedges and fresh parsley, for garnish

Directions:

1. Preheat the oven to 400 degrees F (200°C).
2. Line a baking sheet with parchment paper.
3. In a small bowl, whisk together the honey, dijon mustard, olive oil, lemon juice, paprika, salt, and pepper until well combined.
4. Place the salmon fillets on the prepared baking sheet, skin side down. Brush the honey mustard sauce over the top of each fillet, coating generously.
5. Bake the salmon for 12-15 minutes, or until the salmon is cooked through and flakes easily with a fork.
6. Remove from the oven and let cool for a few minutes before serving.
7. Garnish with lemon wedges and fresh parsley.

Cajun Baked Salmon

Ingredients:

1 lb salmon fillet
1 tbsp olive oil
1 tbsp Cajun seasoning
1 tsp paprika
1/2 tsp garlic powder
Salt and pepper, to taste

Directions:

1. Preheat your oven to 375 degrees F.
2. Line a baking dish with parchment paper.
3. Pat dry the salmon fillet with paper towels.
4. In a small bowl, mix together the olive oil, Cajun seasoning, paprika, garlic powder, salt, and pepper.
5. Rub the mixture all over the salmon fillet, making sure it's evenly coated.
6. Place the salmon fillet in the prepared baking dish.
7. Bake for 12-15 minutes, or until the salmon is cooked through and flakes easily with a fork.
8. Serve hot and enjoy!

Garlic Herb Baked Salmon

Ingredients:

1 lb salmon fillet
1/4 cup olive oil
4 cloves garlic, minced
2 tbsp fresh parsley, chopped
2 tbsp fresh dill, chopped
Salt and pepper to taste
Lemon wedges for serving

Directions:

1. Preheat your oven to 400 degrees F (200°C) and line a baking sheet with parchment paper.
2. Place the salmon fillet on the prepared baking sheet and season with salt and pepper.
3. In a small bowl, whisk together the olive oil, garlic, parsley, and dill.
4. Spoon the herb mixture over the salmon, making sure it's evenly coated.
5. Bake the salmon for 12-15 minutes, or until it flakes easily with a fork.
6. Serve with lemon wedges on the side.

Grilled Salmon Tacos with Avocado Salsa

Ingredients:

1 lb salmon fillet, skin removed
2 tbsp olive oil
1 tsp chili powder
1 tsp garlic powder
1 tsp smoked paprika
1/2 tsp salt
1/4 tsp black pepper
8 corn tortillas
1 avocado, diced
1/2 red onion, diced
1 jalapeno, diced
1/4 cup chopped cilantro
Juice of 1 lime

Directions:

1. Preheat grill to medium-high heat.
2. In a small bowl, mix together olive oil, chili powder, garlic powder, smoked paprika, salt, and black pepper.
3. Brush the spice mixture on both sides of the salmon fillet.
4. Place the salmon fillet on the grill and cook for 5-7 minutes per side, or until the internal temperature of the salmon reaches 145 degrees F.
5. While the salmon is cooking, prepare the avocado salsa.
6. In a medium bowl, combine diced avocado, red onion, jalapeno, cilantro, and lime juice.
7. Warm the corn tortillas on the grill for 30 seconds on each side.
8. Once the salmon is cooked, remove it from the grill and flake it into bite-sized pieces.
9. Assemble the tacos by filling each tortilla with salmon and avocado salsa.
10. Serve immediately and enjoy!

Crispy Salmon Tacos with Chipotle Slaw

Ingredients:

1 lb salmon fillet, skin removed
1 tsp smoked paprika
1/2 tsp cumin
Salt and pepper to taste
1 cup flour
2 eggs, beaten
2 cups panko breadcrumbs
1/4 cup vegetable oil
8-10 corn tortillas
For the slaw:
2 cups shredded cabbage
1/4 cup chopped cilantro
1/4 cup mayonnaise
2 tbsp chipotle hot sauce
2 tbsp lime juice
Salt and pepper to taste

Directions:

1. Preheat the oven to 400 degrees F.
2. In a small bowl, combine the smoked paprika, cumin, salt, and pepper.
3. Season the salmon fillet with the spice mixture.
4. Place the flour, beaten eggs, and panko breadcrumbs in three separate bowls.
5. Coat the salmon fillet in the flour, shaking off any excess.
6. Dip the salmon fillet in the beaten eggs, then coat with the panko breadcrumbs, pressing the breadcrumbs onto the salmon to adhere.
7. Heat the vegetable oil in
8. a large skillet over medium-high heat.
9. Cook the salmon fillet for 2-3 minutes on each side, until crispy and golden brown.

10. Remove the salmon fillet from the skillet and place on a baking sheet lined with parchment paper.
11. Bake in the preheated oven for 10-12 minutes, or until the salmon is cooked through.
12. While the salmon is baking, prepare the slaw by combining the shredded cabbage, cilantro, mayonnaise, chipotle hot sauce, lime juice, salt, and pepper in a large bowl.
13. Heat the corn tortillas on a skillet over medium heat until warm.
14. To assemble the tacos, place a spoonful of the chipotle slaw onto each tortilla, then top with a piece of crispy salmon.
15. Serve immediately.

Blackened Salmon Tacos with Mango Salsa

Ingredients:

4 salmon fillets
1 tbsp. paprika
1 tsp. garlic powder
1 tsp. onion powder
1 tsp. cumin
1/2 tsp. cayenne pepper
Salt and pepper to taste
8 small corn tortillas
1 ripe mango, peeled and diced
1/4 red onion, diced
1/4 cup chopped fresh cilantro
1 tbsp. lime juice
1 tbsp. honey
1 tbsp. olive oil

Directions:

1. Preheat grill to medium-high heat.
2. In a small bowl, mix together paprika, garlic powder, onion powder, cumin, cayenne pepper, salt, and pepper.
3. Rub spice mixture all over the salmon fillets.
4. Grill salmon fillets for 5-6 minutes per side, or until cooked through.
5. While the salmon is cooking, make the mango salsa.
6. In a medium bowl, combine the diced mango, red onion, cilantro, lime juice, honey, and olive oil.
7. Warm the tortillas in the microwave or on the grill.
8. To assemble the tacos, place a piece of salmon on each tortilla and top with mango salsa.
9. Serve immediately.

Teriyaki Salmon Tacos with Pineapple Salsa

Ingredients:

1 lb salmon fillet, skin removed
8-10 small corn tortillas
1 cup chopped fresh pineapple
1 small red onion, diced
1 red bell pepper, diced
1/4 cup chopped fresh cilantro
1 jalapeño, seeded and diced
2 tbsps. rice vinegar
2 tbsps. soy sauce
1 tbsp. honey
1 tbsp. cornstarch
1 tsp. sesame oil
1 tsp. grated ginger
1 garlic clove, minced

Directions:

1. Preheat the oven to 400 degrees F.
2. In a small bowl, whisk together the rice vinegar, soy sauce, honey, cornstarch, sesame oil, ginger, and garlic until well combined.
3. Cut the salmon fillet into small bite-sized pieces and place them on a baking sheet lined with parchment paper.
4. Brush the teriyaki sauce onto the salmon pieces.
5. Bake for 10-12 minutes, or until the salmon is cooked through and flakes easily with a fork.
6. While the salmon is cooking, prepare the pineapple salsa.
7. In a medium bowl, combine the pineapple, red onion, red bell pepper, cilantro, and jalapeño.
8. Warm the tortillas on a hot skillet or grill for 30 seconds on each side.

9. To assemble the tacos, place some salmon pieces on each tortilla, top with pineapple salsa, and serve immediately.

Baja-Style Salmon Tacos with Cabbage Slaw

Ingredients:

1 lb salmon fillet
2 tbsp olive oil
1 tbsp chili powder
1 tsp ground cumin
1 tsp smoked paprika
1/2 tsp garlic powder
1/2 tsp onion powder
Salt and pepper
8 corn tortillas
1 cup shredded cabbage
1/4 cup chopped fresh cilantro
1 lime, cut into wedges
For the sauce:
1/2 cup plain Greek yogurt
2 tbsp mayonnaise
1 tbsp lime juice
1 tsp honey
1/2 tsp ground cumin
Salt and pepper

Directions:

1. Preheat the oven to 375 degrees F (190°C).
2. Line a baking sheet with parchment paper.
3. In a small bowl, mix together the chili powder, cumin, smoked paprika, garlic powder, onion powder, salt, and pepper.
4. Rub the salmon fillet with olive oil, then sprinkle with the spice mixture.
5. Place the salmon on the prepared baking sheet and bake for 15-20 minutes, until cooked through and flaky.

6. While the salmon is cooking, make the sauce by mixing together the Greek yogurt, mayonnaise, lime juice, honey, cumin, salt, and pepper in a small bowl.
7. In a separate bowl, mix together the shredded cabbage and chopped cilantro.
8. Warm the corn tortillas in the microwave or on a griddle.
9. Assemble the tacos by placing a piece of salmon on each tortilla, topping with the cabbage slaw, and drizzling with the sauce.
10. Serve with lime wedges on the side.

Creamy Salmon Pasta

Ingredients:

8 oz. spaghetti
2 tbsp. butter
1 lb. salmon, cut into small pieces
Salt and pepper
2 garlic cloves, minced
1 cup heavy cream
1/2 cup grated Parmesan cheese
1/4 cup chopped fresh parsley

Directions:

1. Cook spaghetti according to package instructions.
2. Melt butter in a large skillet over medium heat.
3. Add salmon and cook until browned on all sides.
4. Season with salt and pepper.
5. Add garlic to the skillet and cook for 1-2 minutes, until fragrant.
6. Pour in heavy cream and bring to a simmer.
7. Cook for 5-7 minutes, stirring occasionally.
8. Stir in Parmesan cheese and parsley.
9. Drain pasta and add it to the skillet.
10. Toss to coat with sauce.

Lemon Garlic Salmon Pasta

Ingredients:

8 oz. spaghetti
1 lb. salmon, cut into small pieces
Salt and pepper
2 garlic cloves, minced
1/4 cup olive oil
1 lemon, zested and juiced
1/4 cup chopped fresh parsley

Directions:

1. Cook spaghetti according to package instructions.
2. Season salmon with salt and pepper.
3. Heat olive oil in a large skillet over medium-high heat.
4. Add salmon and cook until browned on all sides.
5. Add garlic to the skillet and cook for 1-2 minutes, until fragrant.
6. Remove skillet from heat and stir in lemon zest and juice.
7. Drain pasta and add it to the skillet.
8. Toss to coat with sauce.
9. Garnish with parsley.

Salmon Alfredo Pasta

Ingredients:

8 oz. fettuccine
1 lb. salmon, cut into small pieces
Salt and pepper
1/4 cup butter
1 cup heavy cream
1/2 cup grated Parmesan cheese
1/4 cup chopped fresh parsley

Directions:

1. Cook fettuccine according to package instructions.
2. Season salmon with salt and pepper.
3. Melt butter in a large skillet over medium heat.
4. Add salmon and cook until browned on all sides.
5. Pour in heavy cream and bring to a simmer.
6. Cook for 5-7 minutes, stirring occasionally.
7. Stir in Parmesan cheese and parsley.
8. Drain pasta and add it to the skillet.
9. Toss to coat with sauce.

Salmon Pesto Pasta

Ingredients:

8 oz. fusilli
1 lb. salmon, cut into small pieces
Salt and pepper
1/4 cup pesto
1/4 cup grated Parmesan cheese

Directions:

1. Cook fusilli according to package instructions.
2. Season salmon with salt and pepper.
3. Heat a large skillet over medium-high heat.
4. Add salmon and cook until browned on all sides.
5. Add pesto to the skillet and stir to coat salmon.
6. Drain pasta and add it to the skillet.
7. Toss to coat with sauce.
8. Sprinkle Parmesan cheese over pasta and serve.

Creamy Salmon and Spinach Pasta

Ingredients:

8 oz. fettuccine pasta
2 tbsp. unsalted butter
2 cloves garlic, minced
2 cups fresh spinach
1/2 cup heavy cream
1/4 cup grated Parmesan cheese
1/4 cup chopped fresh parsley
1 tbsp. lemon juice
Salt and pepper, to taste
8 oz. cooked salmon, flaked

Directions:

1. Cook the fettuccine pasta according to package instructions until al dente.
2. Drain and set aside.
3. In a large skillet, melt the butter over medium heat.
4. Add the minced garlic and sauté for 1-2 minutes until fragrant.
5. Add the spinach to the skillet and sauté until wilted, about 2-3 minutes.
6. Pour in the heavy cream and grated Parmesan cheese.
7. Stir until the cheese is melted and the sauce is smooth.
8. Add the cooked fettuccine to the skillet and toss until the pasta is coated in the sauce.
9. Stir in the chopped parsley and lemon juice.
10. Season with salt and pepper to taste.
11. Gently fold in the flaked salmon and cook until heated through.
12. Serve immediately.

Creamy Salmon and Broccoli Pasta

Ingredients:

8 oz pasta (penne, fusilli, or any preferred shape)
8 oz fresh salmon fillet, skin removed and cut into small pieces
1 cup broccoli florets
2 tbsp butter
2 cloves garlic, minced
1 cup heavy cream
1/2 cup grated Parmesan cheese
2 tbsp chopped fresh parsley
Salt and pepper to taste

Directions:

1. Cook pasta according to package instructions.
2. Drain and set aside.
3. In a large skillet, melt the butter over medium-high heat.
4. Add garlic and cook for 30 seconds or until fragrant.
5. Add salmon and cook until lightly browned, about 3-4 minutes.
6. Add broccoli and continue cooking for another 2-3 minutes or until it's cooked but still slightly crunchy.
7. Pour in heavy cream and bring to a simmer.
8. Let it cook for 3-4 minutes or until slightly thickened.
9. Add Parmesan cheese, salt, and pepper.
10. Stir until the cheese is melted and the sauce is well combined.
11. Add the cooked pasta to the skillet and toss until coated with the sauce.
12. Serve hot, topped with chopped parsley.

Salmon Linguine

Ingredients:

8 oz. linguine pasta
2 cloves garlic, chopped
2 tbsps. olive oil
2 medium fresh tomatoes, diced
8 oz. cooked salmon, flaked
1/4 cup white wine
Salt and pepper to taste
Pinch of red pepper flakes (optional)
Fresh parsley for garnish

Directions:

1. Cook linguine according to package directions until al dente.
2. In a separate pan, sauté chopped garlic in olive oil over medium heat until fragrant, for about 1-2 minutes.
3. Add diced fresh tomatoes to the pan and continue cooking for about 5-7 minutes, until they have softened.
4. Add cooked, flaked salmon and white wine to the pan and continue cooking for 2-3 minutes until the salmon is heated through.
5. Season with salt, pepper, and red pepper flakes, if desired.
6. Drain the linguine and add it to the pan with the salmon sauce.
7. Toss until the pasta is coated evenly.
8. Serve hot and garnish with fresh parsley. Enjoy your delicious Salmon Linguine!

Salmon Carbonara

Ingredients:

8 oz spaghetti
4 oz pancetta, diced
2 cloves garlic, minced
2 egg yolks
1/2 cup grated Parmesan cheese
8 oz cooked salmon, flaked
Black pepper
Chopped fresh parsley for garnish

Directions:

1. Cook spaghetti according to package directions.
2. Drain and set aside.
3. In a separate pan, sauté diced pancetta until crispy.
4. Add minced garlic and continue to cook until fragrant.
5. In a small bowl, whisk together egg yolks and grated Parmesan cheese.
6. Remove the pan from the heat and add the drained spaghetti to the pancetta and garlic.
7. Quickly toss in the egg yolk mixture, being careful not to scramble the eggs.
8. Flake in cooked salmon and season with black pepper.
9. Toss everything together until the salmon is warmed through.
10. Garnish with chopped fresh parsley and serve hot.

Cedar Plank Salmon with Brown Sugar Glaze

Ingredients:

1 cedar plank
1/4 cup brown sugar
1/4 cup Dijon mustard
1/4 cup soy sauce
1 tbsp olive oil
2 garlic cloves, minced
1 tsp ground ginger
1 tsp black pepper
4 (6 oz) salmon fillets

Directions:

1. Soak the cedar plank in water for at least 1 hour before cooking.
2. Preheat the grill to medium-high heat.
3. In a small bowl, whisk together the brown sugar, Dijon mustard, soy sauce, olive oil, garlic, ginger, and black pepper.
4. Place the salmon fillets on the cedar plank and brush them generously with the glaze.
5. Place the cedar plank on the grill and close the lid.
6. Cook for 12-15 minutes, or until the salmon is cooked through and flakes easily with a fork.

Cedar Plank Salmon with Lemon Herb Butter

Ingredients:

1 cedar plank
4 (6 oz) salmon fillets
1/2 cup unsalted butter, softened
1 lemon, zested and juiced
1 tbsp chopped fresh thyme
1 tbsp chopped fresh rosemary
1 tsp salt
1/2 tsp black pepper

Directions:

1. Soak the cedar plank in water for at least 1 hour before cooking.
2. Preheat the grill to medium-high heat.
3. In a small bowl, combine the softened butter, lemon zest, lemon juice, thyme, rosemary, salt, and black pepper.
4. Place the salmon fillets on the cedar plank and spread the lemon herb butter over the top.
5. Place the cedar plank on the grill and close the lid.
6. Cook for 12-15 minutes, or until the salmon is cooked through and flakes easily with a fork.

Lemon Garlic Cedar Plank Salmon

Ingredients:

1 cedar plank
1 1/2 pounds salmon fillet
2 cloves garlic, minced
1/4 cup olive oil
1/4 cup lemon juice
1/4 tsp. salt
1/4 tsp. black pepper
1 lemon, thinly sliced

Directions:

1. Soak cedar plank in water for at least 2 hours.
2. Preheat grill to medium-high heat.
3. In a bowl, whisk together garlic, olive oil, lemon juice, salt, and black pepper.
4. Place the salmon fillet on the soaked cedar plank and brush the garlic mixture over the top.
5. Place the lemon slices on top of the salmon.
6. Place the cedar plank on the grill and close the lid.
7. Cook for 15-20 minutes, or until the salmon is cooked through and flakes easily with a fork.

Cedar Plank Salmon with Honey Mustard Glaze

Ingredients:

1 cedar plank
4 (6 oz) salmon fillets
1/4 cup honey
2 tbsp Dijon mustard
1 tbsp apple cider vinegar
1 tsp smoked paprika
1 tsp salt
1/2 tsp black pepper

Directions:

1. Soak the cedar plank in water for at least 1 hour before cooking.
2. Preheat the grill to medium-high heat.
3. In a small bowl, whisk together the honey, Dijon mustard, apple cider vinegar, smoked paprika, salt, and black pepper.
4. Place the salmon fillets on the cedar plank and brush them generously with the honey mustard glaze.
5. Place the cedar plank on the grill and close the lid.
6. Cook for 12-15 minutes, or until the salmon is cooked through and flakes easily with a fork.

Maple Glazed Cedar Plank Salmon

Ingredients:

1 cedar plank
1 1/2 pounds salmon fillet
1/4 cup maple syrup
1/4 cup soy sauce
2 tbsps. olive oil
2 cloves garlic, minced
1/2 tsp. black pepper
1/4 tsp. salt

Directions:

1. Soak cedar plank in water for at least 2 hours.
2. Preheat grill to medium-high heat.
3. In a bowl, whisk together maple syrup, soy sauce, olive oil, garlic, salt, and black pepper.
4. Place the salmon fillet on the soaked cedar plank and brush the maple mixture over the top.
5. Place the cedar plank on the grill and close the lid.
6. Cook for 15-20 minutes, or until the salmon is cooked through and flakes easily with a fork.

Smoky Cedar Plank Salmon

Ingredients:

1 cedar plank
1 1/2 pounds salmon fillet
1 tbsp. smoked paprika
1/2 tsp. garlic powder
1/4 tsp. salt
1/4 tsp. black pepper
2 tbsps. olive oil

Directions:

1. Soak cedar plank in water for at least 2 hours.
2. Preheat grill to medium-high heat.
3. In a bowl, mix together smoked paprika, garlic powder, salt, black pepper, and olive oil.
4. Place the salmon fillet on the soaked cedar plank and rub the spice mixture over the top.
5. Place the cedar plank on the grill and close the lid.
6. Cook for 15-20 minutes, or until the salmon is cooked through and flakes easily with a fork.

Teriyaki Cedar Plank Salmon

Ingredients:

1 cedar plank, soaked in water for 1-2 hours
4 salmon fillets
1/2 cup teriyaki sauce
1/4 cup soy sauce
2 tbsps. honey
2 tbsps. rice vinegar
2 cloves garlic, minced
1 tsp. grated fresh ginger
1/4 tsp. red pepper flakes
Sliced green onions and sesame seeds, for garnish

Directions:

1. Preheat the grill to medium-high heat.
2. In a small bowl, whisk together the teriyaki sauce, soy sauce, honey, rice vinegar, garlic, ginger, and red pepper flakes.
3. Place the soaked cedar plank on the grill and let it heat up for 2-3 minutes.
4. Place the salmon fillets on the cedar plank, skin-side down.
5. Brush the teriyaki sauce mixture generously over the salmon.
6. Close the lid of the grill and let the salmon cook for 12-15 minutes, or until cooked through.
7. Remove the cedar plank from the grill and let the salmon rest for a few minutes.
8. Garnish with sliced green onions and sesame seeds before serving.

Spicy Cedar Plank Salmon

Ingredients:

1 cedar plank
1 1/2 pounds salmon fillet
2 tbsps. olive oil
2 tbsps. brown sugar
1 tbsp. smoked paprika
1 tsp. garlic powder
1 tsp. onion powder
1 tsp. cumin
1 tsp. chili powder
1 tsp. salt
1/2 tsp. black pepper

Directions:

1. Soak the cedar plank in water for at least 1 hour.
2. Preheat the grill to medium-high heat.
3. In a small bowl, mix together the olive oil, brown sugar, smoked paprika, garlic powder, onion powder, cumin, chili powder, salt, and black pepper.
4. Place the salmon fillet on the cedar plank, skin-side down.
5. Brush the spice mixture over the salmon, covering it evenly.
6. Place the cedar plank on the grill and close the lid.
7. Cook the salmon for 15-20 minutes, or until it flakes easily with a fork and the internal temperature reaches 145 degrees F.
8. Carefully remove the cedar plank from the grill and transfer the salmon to a serving platter.
9. Garnish with chopped fresh cilantro or green onions, if desired.

Chile Garlic BBQ Salmon

Ingredients:

1 cedar plank
1 1/2 lb salmon fillet
1/4 cup chili garlic sauce
2 tbsp soy sauce
2 tbsp honey
1 tbsp lime juice
1 tbsp olive oil
2 cloves garlic, minced
Salt and pepper

Directions:

1. Soak the cedar plank in water for at least 1 hour.
2. Preheat the grill to medium-high heat.
3. In a small bowl, whisk together chili garlic sauce, soy sauce, honey, lime juice, olive oil, and minced garlic.
4. Season the salmon fillet with salt and pepper, then place it on the soaked cedar plank.
5. Brush the chili garlic sauce mixture over the top of the salmon fillet.
6. Place the cedar plank with the salmon on the grill and close the lid.
7. Cook for 10-15 minutes or until the salmon is cooked through and flakes easily with a fork.
8. Serve with additional chili garlic sauce on top, if desired.

Chile Garlic BBQ Salmon

Ingredients:

1 cedar plank
1 1/2 lb salmon fillet
1/4 cup chili garlic sauce
2 tbsp soy sauce
2 tbsp honey
1 tbsp lime juice
1 tbsp olive oil
2 cloves garlic, minced
Salt and pepper

Directions:

1. Soak the cedar plank in water for at least 1 hour.
2. Preheat the grill to medium-high heat.
3. In a small bowl, whisk together chili garlic sauce, soy sauce, honey, lime juice, olive oil, and minced garlic.
4. Season the salmon fillet with salt and pepper, then place it on the soaked cedar plank.
5. Brush the chili garlic sauce mixture over the top of the salmon fillet.
6. Place the cedar plank with the salmon on the grill and close the lid.
7. Cook for 10-15 minutes or until the salmon is cooked through and flakes easily with a fork.
8. Serve with additional chili garlic sauce on top, if desired.

Fennel-Smoked Salmon

Ingredients:

1 whole salmon fillet (about 2 pounds)
2 tbsps. fennel seeds
1 tbsp. sea salt
1 tbsp. freshly ground black pepper
2 tbsps. olive oil
2 tbsps. lemon juice

Directions:

1. Soak a cedar plank in water for at least 1 hour.
2. Rinse the salmon fillet and pat it dry with paper towels.
3. Place it on a cutting board, skin-side down.
4. In a small bowl, mix the fennel seeds, sea salt, and black pepper. Rub the spice mixture all over the salmon fillet.
5. Preheat your grill or oven to 400 degrees F (200°C).
6. Place the soaked cedar plank on the grill or on a baking sheet in the oven for 5-10 minutes until it begins to smoke.
7. Brush the salmon fillet with olive oil and transfer it to the cedar plank, skin-side down.
8. Place the plank on the grill or in the oven and cook for about 15-20 minutes, or until the salmon is cooked through and flakes easily with a fork.
9. Remove the plank from the grill or oven and let it cool for a few minutes.
10. Drizzle the lemon juice over the cooked salmon and serve.

About the Author

Laura Sommers is **The Recipe Lady!**

She lives on a small farm in Baltimore County, Maryland and has a passion for food. She has taken cooking classes in New York City, Memphis, New Orleans and Washington DC. She has been a taste tester for a large spice company in Baltimore and written food reviews for several local papers. She loves writing cookbooks with the most delicious recipes to share her knowledge and love of cooking with the world.

Follow her on Pinterest:

http://pinterest.com/therecipelady1

Visit the Recipe Lady's blog for even more great recipes:

http://the-recipe-lady.blogspot.com/

Visit her Amazon Author Page to see her latest books:

amazon.com/author/laurasommers

Follow the Recipe Lady on Facebook:

https://www.facebook.com/therecipegirl

Follow her on Twitter:

https://twitter.com/TheRecipeLady1

Other Books by Laura Sommers

Irish Recipes for St. Patrick's Day

Traditional Vermont Recipes

Traditional Memphis Recipes

Maryland Chesapeake Bay Blue Crab Cookbook

Mussels Cookbook

Maryland Chesapeake Bay Blue Crab Cookbook

Salmon Cookbook

Scallop Recipes